T0131733

Angels Surrounding Me

Dierdre A. Shelton

AuthorHouse™
1663 Liberty Drive
Bloomington, IN 47403
www.authorhouse.com
Phone: 833-262-8899

Because of the dynamic nature of the Internet, any web addresses or links contained in this book may have changed
since publication and may no longer be valid. The views expressed in this work are solely those of the author and do
not necessarily reflect the views of the publisher, and the publisher hereby disclaims any responsibility for them.

Any people depicted in stock imagery provided by Getty Images are models,
and such images are being used for illustrative purposes only.
Certain stock imagery © Getty Images.

This is a work of fiction. All of the characters, names, incidents, organizations, and dialogue in
this novel are either the products of the author's imagination or are used fictitiously.

This book is printed on acid-free paper.

ISBN: 978-1-4389-4407-4 (sc)
ISBN: 978-1-4772-0161-9 (e)

Library of Congress Control Number: 2009900162

Print information available on the last page.

Published by AuthorHouse 02/09/2022

authorHOUSE

In Memory of

Earnest James Shelton
Lorene Young
Curtis Reed
Bertha Shelton

Acknowledgments

First and foremost, giving God all of the Glory for placing this

work in me and using me as His vessel.

Minister Sylvia Dandridge

Thank you for your prayers, spiritual guidance, and

encouragement.

Loretta Shelton

Thank you for your words of wisdom.

Karen Chaplin, M.D.

Thank you for your motivation and encouragement.

Denise W. Moore

Thank you for your graciousness and editorial comments.

Ruth A. White

Thank you for allowing God to stretch you and use you to bring

this work to life so that He may receive all of the glory.

Do you believe in angels? I do. Do you have angels? I do. Let me tell you a story about how God sent four angels to help my family and me when my mother was diagnosed with cancer. My name is Kingston James Reed and I am six years old. My mother told me that Kingston means that I am an heir to the Son of the King, Jesus Christ. James is my grandfather's middle name, and Reed is my great-grandfather's last name.

(Psalm 34:7, Luke 4:10, Matthew 18:10)

First, let me tell you about my mommy. I have to say there is something special about her. She is sooo beautiful to me. Her hair is soft and pretty. Her skin is like caramel candy and feels like satiny sheets. Her big sparkling eyes greet me every morning, and her smile makes me happy when I am sad. Mommy's voice is like music gently waking me up in the morning. Each morning, we would say hello to God, by saying a prayer, before we did anything else. It went something like this: "Good morning, God! Thank you for waking me up. Thank you for being my Heavenly Father. Thank you for creating me in Christ Jesus for good works. Thank you for giving me great blessings. I have everything because I have Christ. Thank you for sending angels to watch over me. I will obey you, God, and my parents too. I will honor my parents for the rest of my life. I will listen and pay attention in school. I will always tell the truth. I am valuable. I am respectful. Jesus is my friend and my example. Amen!"

(Ephesians 1:3, 5-6, Ephesians 2:10, Ephesians 3:6, Proverbs 6:20-23)

After we said our morning prayer, I ate my breakfast. Mommy made my hot cereal smooth and creamy. Yummy, yummy, yummy. What a happy tummy!

Once a week, my daddy took me to school on his way to work. We did not say much, but I liked spending this time with him. Mommy called this our "guy time." Daddy would say a prayer before we started driving, so that we'd get to school safely, and he would say, "Thank you, Jesus," when we arrived at school or any other declaration. Oh, one of my angels has corrected me… I meant to say… any other **destination**.

Mommy included Jesus in everything we did, too. We would thank Jesus when we got in the car, when we got out of the car, and even when we walked through our front door. Jesus is good because He makes sure His angels keep us safe.

One day Mommy went to see her doctor after she dropped me off at school. Now that I think about it, she just didn't seem the same that day. When she picked me up from school, she really didn't look too good either. I thought of different ways to cheer her up, but none of them seemed to work. I told her that Daddy would make it all right. She seemed divided or subtracted, whatever the grown-up people say when people are not really paying attention, because of something else on their minds. Oh, I have been corrected by another angel. She seemed **distracted**. I thought about how to make her feel better. I told her that God is always with her and His angels will always be surrounding her and cheering for her happiness. She gave me a small smile and said, "If you only knew how true that is, spoken in innocence, but yet so true." Then she said something that I really didn't understand. She said, "Out of the mouths of babes." I thought to myself, "Humph, I am not a baby. I don't wear diapers anymore."

(Psalm 8:2)

Daddy met us at the front door. I thought Mommy would be a little happier, seeing Daddy waiting on us. As soon as she walked inside the house, she started crying. My daddy hugged her and then he started crying. Everybody was crying. I didn't know what to do, because I didn't know what they were crying about. I tried to help them by giving them both a hug, and I started crying. If someone else had walked into our home during this time, they would have started crying too.

The next few weeks, Mommy went to see her doctor a lot. Some days, I really had to look hard to see the mother I knew. She needed a lot of rest. After she got her rest, she seemed like her old self again. Sometimes she did not want to eat. She said the food did not have a taste. This is when she started losing weight. She prayed a lot, and sometimes, we all prayed together. I would pray in my head when I looked at my mother, but she didn't know it. Daddy didn't know it either. Sometimes, I tried to pray without squinting my eyes, but it was hard. I just tried to act like I was thinking about something. I guess it didn't work, because a few times, Mommy asked me if my head was hurting or if I was sick. We also listened to a lot of Gospel music during this time.

Suddenly, Mommy got better. Daddy said prayer changes things. I believe it, because Mommy looked just like the Mommy that I used to know. We started taking lots of fun trips. We went to Disneyworld and to the Animal Kingdom. We did other fun things like flying kites, roller skating, and ice skating. One day we all went horseback riding. Now that was really cool. That horse was a big animal for a little person like me to ride. I was a little scared, but I was also excited. That was one day I said, "Thank you, Jesus!" when I got back on the ground safely. My mother seemed to have had as much fun as I did. Daddy didn't do too badly either.

I don't know what I would do without my mother and father, because they are so special to me. I have a lot of aunts, uncles, and cousins, and we always spend Sundays and holidays together. I have to admit, for the longest time I did not realize that they were all related to me. I just thought that we were going to visit my mother's friends. Now that I think about it, it seemed like every Sunday was a family reunion. Well, I guess it was. It really feels good to be in a family like mine.

    A lot of time has gone by since my mother first became sick. Mommy started getting sick again right after Christmas. It was like Day John Rules. Oh, I have been corrected by one of my angels. It was like ***déjà vu***. We all started crying again just like the last time, except this time, Mommy was at home waiting on Daddy and me. This time, we all got on our knees and started praying for a healing. They were praying for a healing—but from what? I didn't know how to ask them. I just figured whatever it was would go away like the time before.

    Mommy was in and out of the hospital more this time than the last time. It seemed like she was going to see her doctor every day. She had her good days where she looked like herself, and she had some bad days too. She seemed to be at peace with whatever was going on with that healing thing. I guess they are right: Prayer works.

One night in January, shortly after the New Year's holiday, while praying to God for Mommy to have peace and healing, I noticed something in the corner of my ceiling. I had just finished saying, "Jesus, Jesus, Jesus." Daddy told me this name changes things and things happen whenever we say the name of Jesus. At first, I was kind of scared and I wanted to run to Mommy's bedroom, but I couldn't move. I focused my eyes and realized that the sight before me was not scary at all. It was an angel. Hey, God sent and angel that kind of looked like my grandfather. Maybe I should ask the angel what type of healing my mother needed. Naw, I thought and just then, the angel smiled at me; he made me feel safe.

I went to sleep and when I woke up, the angel was still there. I ran and got my Daddy and told him to come to my bedroom. I wanted him to see the angel. He would be happy to know that I had an angel in my room. Daddy came into my room, but he did not see the angel. The angel was still there, so I ran to Mommy and Daddy's bedroom and I noticed that an angel was in their bedroom also. I told Daddy to come back to his room; he went in but he did not see the angel.

One day, I asked Mommy to come to my bedroom and I showed her the angel. Guess what? She said that she saw the angel too. We went to her bedroom and she saw the angel there as well! For a minute, I was beginning to think I was seeing things. She told me that it was good to have angels watching over us. I wondered why Daddy couldn't see the angel.

Snow fell on the ground in February. Mommy was able to come out on the porch to watch Daddy and me play in the snow. She also helped me throw a few snowballs at him. These days, she got tired quickly, so she went back inside and watched us play from the window. After we finished our playing in the snow, Mommy had hot chocolate waiting for us when we came inside. Boy, what a fun time we had today! Mommy tried to look happy, but she also looked sad. Maybe she's just weak.

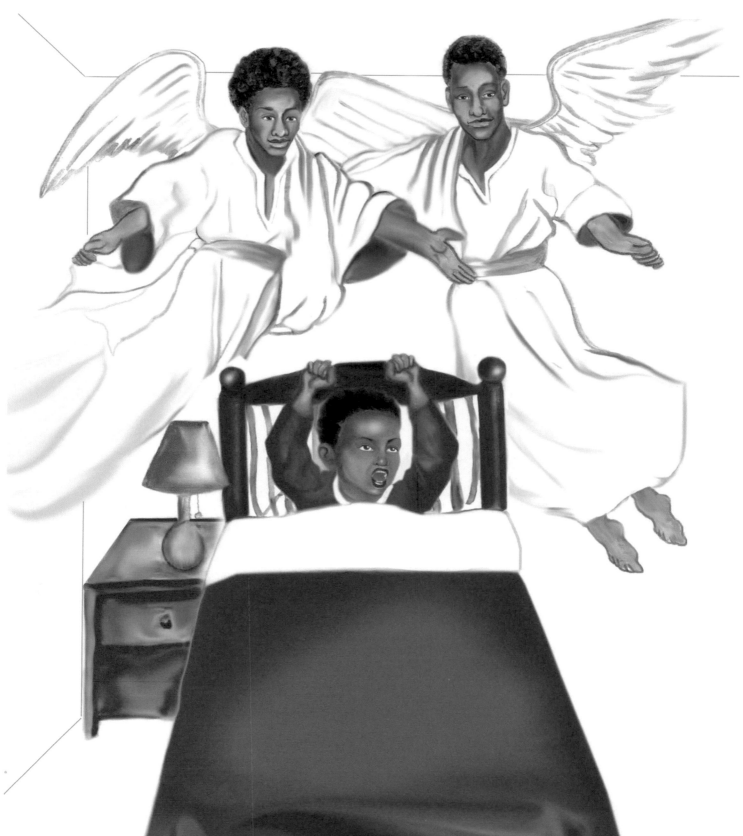

That night, I called the name "Jesus, Jesus, Jesus," as I prayed for Mommy to have protection and healing, and then I went to sleep. When I woke up, I noticed God sent another angel. This angel was just as handsome and nice as the first angel. He was perched in the opposite corner of the first angel.

They both smiled at each other and then they smiled at me. I ran to my parents' bedroom. Another angel was in there too. After Daddy left the room, I asked Mommy if she saw the second angel. I didn't want to ask her in front of Daddy because I did not want him to feel left out. Yes, she told me that she saw the second angel as well. Mommy told me that this signals that we have received a double portion of God's blessings. We have two angels watching over us and we can see them! I wondered why Daddy couldn't see the angels. He believes in God. He is saved and he prays.

Mommy seemed to be doing well in March, although she was still seeing her doctor a lot. The birds were chirping, the snow was melting, and the sun was shining. Things seemed so fresh and new. Suddenly, Mommy started losing her hair, and eventually, she lost all of her hair. I did not mind because she was my Mommy and she still looked beautiful to me. I kind of liked it. She started wearing some other hair on her head. They call that a wig.

By now, my prayers were stronger, and I was praying harder and harder. I prayed for security and healing. You are not going to believe this: I had just finished saying "Jesus, Jesus, Jesus," and guess what? God sent a third angel to my bedroom. The angels smiled at each other and then they smiled at me. Again, I ran into my parents' bedroom and there was a third angel in their bedroom. I could not tell if the angels that I saw in my bedroom were the same angels that I saw in their bedroom. Well, I thought I would find out by taking a picture of them. So, I took pictures in both rooms but the angels did not show up in the pictures. "Now what am I going to do?"

I never tried talking to the angels. Hmmm…I guess I'll have to try talking to the angels now. I have to find out why they are here. I have to find out why Mommy and I are the only ones that can see them. I know that God sent them, because they appeared right after I prayed and said, "Jesus, Jesus, Jesus."

"Angels, why are you here?" I asked. The first angel said, "I was sent for your peace. When your mother got sick the second time, you asked for her to have peace and healing in your prayers." The second angel said, "I was sent for your protection. When you prayed for your mother, you asked for her to have protection and healing." The third angel said, "I was sent for your security. When you prayed the third time, you asked for security and healing. You said that you did not know what you would do without your parents. I am here to let you know that God is with you whether your parents are around you or not. You will be secure in God. You will be confident, because of God." The angels said a lot that I had to think about. Wow! They knew my prayers.

Mommy started going to the hospital a lot. Most of the time, she was too weak to play with me or laugh when she returned home. Sometimes, she gave me a weak smile. I really felt bad for her. One day they sent Mommy to a place for sick people called a hospice. They said they could not do anything for her. I thought, "Well, maybe the doctors cannot do anything, but God can sure do something." So I got on my knees and prayed again. I prayed that God would bring Mommy through this again. I missed seeing her the way that she used to be. Some days I didn't think she knew me.

Finally, Mommy came home from the hospice. She did not look so good. I tried to talk to her, but she was sleeping a lot. I went to my bedroom and sat in the middle of my bed and began praying. This time, I began my prayer with "Jesus, Jesus, Jesus," and ended my prayer with "Jesus, Jesus, Jesus." God sent another angel who appeared in the fourth corner of my bedroom! Yep. You know what I did? I ran to my parents' bedroom. There was a fourth angel in their bedroom as well. I asked this angel why he was here. The fourth angel said that he was sent to comfort me. Comfort? I was going to ask him what that meant. The angel answered my question before I could ask him. The angel said "comfort" means to bring relief from grief or sorrow; to ease pain; to make life easy or comfortable. I didn't have pain. I was not feeling sad or sorry about anything. I just felt bad that my mother had to go through all of that again. I wondered what he was talking about. He heard my thoughts again. He said, "You will understand later."

My grandmother and aunts came to see us and spent a lot of time with my mother. They looked very sad. It seemed to me they needed the "Comforter Angel."

I talked to Mommy on the last day of winter. She smiled at me so beautifully. Her face was peaceful. I felt so protected and I was also at peace. Her touch seemed to be like a feather. Right at that moment, I was confident that everything would be okay. I looked up at each of the four corners of the bedroom walls and the angels were looking at me. They did make me feel peaceful, protected, and secure. I guess I have to wait to find out about comfort.

That night, we all went to bed. I looked up at my ceiling, and the angels were surrounding me. I had a dream that Mommy was in the center of my bedroom above me. Her soft curly hair was back on her head and she looked like her old self again. She was happy and healthy and more beautiful than ever. Mommy took me to a beautiful place that was green and peaceful and there were a lot of waterfalls. We laughed, played, and danced together; we even sang songs. We had sooo much fun!

She talked to me about life and her expectations of me, as a boy, as a man, as a husband, and as a father. She told me so much. I told her I didn't know if I could remember it all. She told me that it would come back to me when I needed it.

Mommy told me a secret about why my daddy could not see the angels. She said that it was simple. Daddy was not ready to see the angels. She told me that sometimes adults cannot see things like kids.

I asked her to tell me about the healing she asked for in her prayers. She told me that she had cancer. I asked her what that meant. She said it was a little complicated, but she would try to make it simple. She told me that everybody has good cells and bad cells in their body, and that the bad cells in her body became stronger and took over the good cells. She also said that her body could not fight it anymore, and this caused her to become weaker and weaker. Her immune system could no longer fight off germs or colds either.

Mommy also told me about the cycle of life. She said everything that is born will eventually die, and there is a time and a season for everything. She told me that she loved me and she would always be with me, but she had to go to another place. I asked her what place. She said, "Heaven." She said God told her that she had been a good and faithful servant. I asked her if she could come back when God was finished with her. She told me no and that she had to obey God and stay in heaven, because she had finished the assignment that God had given her here on earth.

(Ecclesiastes 3:1-8)

She told me that the angels in my bedroom and in her bedroom are the same angels. I knew it! They were protecting her and letting me know that I was protected as well. She said that I am young and I needed something that I could see to make me understand that God will always be here for me. She also told me that the angels would always surround me.

Mommy kissed me on my cheek and told me not to worry about her. She said that she would be in a good place with God. She told me that

I would join her one day, but only when God said that my assignment here on earth was over. She said that I could not come to heaven before God told me to come to Him. She said that anybody who accepted Jesus Christ as their Lord and Savior could go to heaven. These people have confessed their sins, and they know that Jesus died for them and rose on the third day, so that they could have eternal life. She said that although a person's earthly life can be taken, their salvation could never be taken away. She added that eternal life is forever and that we are only on earth temporarily. Mommy told me everything that I needed to know about this life and eternal life. This was a lot for me to understand. We both decided to go to sleep. I think she went to sleep first. She looked so beautiful and so peaceful. She had a smile on her face that I will never forget.

When I woke up the Angel of Comfort was sitting in the middle of my bed. I looked at the other corners and the other angels were still there. I got ready to jump out of bed to look in Mommy and Daddy's bedroom. The Angel of Comfort told me to be still for a minute. He pointed out that the Angels of Peace, Protection, and Security would always be with me. He told me that he was here now to walk with me, hold me, hug me, cry with me, and comfort me. He told me that my mother was now in heaven. He said her physical body was still in her bedroom, but her spiritual body was in heaven with God.

When I went into Mommy and Daddy's bedroom, Daddy was kneeling beside my mother with his eyes closed. Tears were streaming down his face. I touched his shoulder and as he looked up at me, I could see that he was sad. I told him to look up at the corner of the wall, and I introduced him to the Angel of Peace. Daddy smiled. Then I introduced him to the Angel of Protection, and then the Angel of Security. I asked Daddy if he saw the angels. He said, "Yes." We hugged each other. I told him that I had to introduce him to one more angel. The Angel of Comfort greeted him. Daddy said that we both were going to need this angel for a while and he told me that God knows what to give us when we need it.

Daddy and I looked at each other and somehow knew that everything was going to be all right. God was with us that day and He is still with us. The angels are there with every step we take.

Dierdre Shelton has written this book for any child facing an unexpected crisis. She wants each child to know they are not forgotten by God. Because God comforted her through her own personal loss, she also wants children to remember that God's angels will always surround them with peace, protection, security, and comfort. May you be blessed, encouraged, and strengthened by this book.

Printed in the United States
by Baker & Taylor Publisher Services